Pebble®

American Shorthair Cats

by Wendy Perkins

Consulting Editor: Gail Saunders-Smith, PhD

Consultant: Jennifer Zablotny, DVM
Member, American Veterinary Medical Association

Capstone
press

Mankato, Minnesota

Pebble Books are published by Capstone Press,
151 Good Counsel Drive, P.O. Box 669, Mankato, Minnesota 56002.
www.capstonepress.com

1 2 3 4 5 6 13 12 11 10 09 08

Library of Congress Cataloging-in-Publication Data
Perkins, Wendy, 1957–.
    American shorthair cats / by Wendy Perkins.
    p. cm. — (Pebble Books. Cats)
    Includes bibliographical references and index.
    ISBN-13: 978-1-4296-1215-9 (hardcover)
    ISBN-10: 1-4296-1215-0 (hardcover)
    1. American shorthair cat — Juvenile literature. I. Title. II. Series.
SF449.A45P47 2008
636.8'22 — dc22   2007017792

Summary: Simple text and photographs present an introduction to the American
Shorthair breed, its growth from kitten to adult, and pet care information.

Note to Parents and Teachers

The Cats set supports national science standards related to life
science. This book describes and illustrates American Shorthair
cats. The images support early readers in understanding the text.
The repetition of words and phrases helps early readers learn new
words. This book also introduces early readers to subject-specific
vocabulary words, which are defined in the Glossary section. Early
readers may need assistance to read some words and to use the
Table of Contents, Glossary, Read More, Internet Sites, and Index
sections of the book.

Table of Contents

Playful Cats

American Shorthair cats
are playful pets.
They like other cats.
American Shorthairs are
even good with dogs.

Most American Shorthairs
are silver, brown,
or orange tabbies.
Tabbies are cats
with striped coats.

Some American Shorthairs
are calicos.
They have patches of
black, white, and
orange fur.

From Kitten to Adult

American Shorthair kittens
run and chase each other.

American Shorthair
kittens use a litter box
as soon as they can walk.

American Shorthair cats
grow quickly.
They are adults after
about one year.

Caring for American Shorthairs

Owners need to feed their American Shorthairs every day.

Hard, crunchy food helps keep their teeth clean.

American Shorthairs
rarely need to be brushed.
Their rough tongues clean off
dirt and loose fur.

American Shorthair cats
are good pets.
They love attention
from their owners.

Glossary

attention — playing, talking, and spending time with a person or animal

calico — a cat with patches of black, white, and orange fur

litter box — a container kept indoors for a cat to go to the bathroom; owners must clean litter boxes every day.

tabby — a cat with a striped coat

Read More

Barnes, Julia. *Pet Cats.* Pet Pals. Milwaukee: Gareth Stevens, 2007.

Furstinger, Nancy. *American Shorthair Cats.* Cats. Set IV. Edina, Minn.: Abdo, 2006.

Ganeri, Anita. *Cats.* Heinemann First Library. A Pet's Life. Chicago: Heinemann, 2003.

Internet Sites

FactHound offers a safe, fun way to find Internet sites related to this book. All of the sites on FactHound have been researched by our staff.

Here's how:

1. Visit *www.facthound.com*

2. Choose your grade level.

3. Type in this book **ID 1429612150** for age-appropriate sites. You may also browse subjects by clicking on letters, or by clicking on pictures and words.

4. Click on the **Fetch It** button.

FactHound will fetch the best sites for you!

Index

Word Count: 124
Grade: 1
Early-Intervention Level: 16

Editorial Credits
Erika L. Shores, editor; Renée T. Doyle, set designer; Veronica Bianchini and Ted Williams, contributing designers; Linda Clavel, photo researcher

Photo Credits
Chanan Photography, cover, 1, 22
Fiona Green, 6, 20
Jewison-Pfeiffer family of Mpls., Mn. 16
Jupiterimages/Creatas Images, 14
Minden Pictures/MITSUAKI IWAGO, 10
Nancy M. McCallum, 4, 12
Ron Kimball Stock/Ron Kimball, 8, 18

Cats on pages 6 and 20, courtesy of Silver 'N Gold cattery, Texas.